ACTIVATE

50 PRINCIPLES THAT WILL
HELP YOU *LEAD WITH CONFIDENCE*

ACTIVATE

50 PRINCIPLES THAT WILL
HELP YOU *LEAD WITH CONFIDENCE*

JESSE A. COLE, JR.

CEDAR HILL
PUBLISHING

Jesse Speaks International, LLC
P.O. Box 442
Hazel Park, Michigan 48030
www.JesseSpeaks.com

ISBN 10: 0984779876
ISBN 13: 978-0984779871

Printed in the United States of America

DEDICATION

This book is dedicated to the those who are aware of their leadership potential, are convinced that they have a purpose, but are searching for the answers to fill in the gaps of their confidence.

"Believe in yourself! Have faith in your abilities! Without a humble but reasonable confidence in your own powers you cannot be successful or happy."

-Norman Vincent Peale

CONTENTS

INTRODUCTION 9

SECTION 1*: CONFIDENCE* 13

SECTION 2: *SPIRUTUAL MATURITY* 25

SECTION 3: *RELATIONSHIPS* 42

SECTION 4: *INFLUENCE* 51

SECTION 5:*VISION & PURPOSE* 62

CONCLUSION.. 80

INTRODUCTION

The inspiration behind this book is the result of a conversation that I had with one my closest ministry colleagues. We were talking about the challenges of being a leader in ministry when he posed an interesting question: "How is it that we know the word of God, can quote scriptures, but very few of us have the confidence to live it out? How do we make the connection between *knowing* and *doing*?"

Hebrews 4:12 says, the word of God is, "...alive and active..." a living organism and a convicting element that, "...penetrates even to dividing soul and spirit, joints and marrow; it judges the thoughts and attitudes of the heart." (NIV).

As leaders we can take a que from this scripture. Our role is to help people become the better version of themselves, and at times that involves challenging them as well as filling in the gaps for them. This is not the same as doing the work for them. That would be counterproductive since leaders are supposed to create leaders, not followers.

Challenging their current state and filling in the gaps requires us to educate and train others to move from their current reality to their desired reality. In doing this, we may disrupt their ideologies, habits and expectations; but the purpose is to encourage our people to engage with the rigor of development which increases their capacity to lead others to their desired reality.

So why did I decide to produce a book like this you ask? Well, it goes back to the conversation I had with my friend. Quoting the word of God means nothing if there is a deficiency in application. I named this book *ACTIVATE* because that's what the word of God is meant to do and that is exactly what I want to help you do. A rocket has all the built-in potential to soar, but for it to launch it must first be activated. In order for you to use your cell phone as it was intended to be used you have to make sure that it is activated. In the early 90's you could buy a phone card with preloaded minutes, but you couldn't use it until you called a designated phone number to activate it.

The difference between you and the items I just mentioned is that in order for them to be used, someone has to push a button to activate them, they can't activate themselves. However, you have the ability to self-activate.

I felt it was necessary to share pieces of my personal notes, speeches, sermons and presentations with you in this palatable format. Each principle has a corresponding scripture to give you spiritual insight on a practical belief. Don't just take the scriptures at face value. I encourage you to delve deeper into the context of each scripture. Doing this will not only increase your understanding of the passage, but will help you appreciate how the correlating principle is relevant to your life. My hope is that you find a piece of yourself in this work; that you become so engulfed in building your confidence that you, as Henry Thoreau once said, "...become the tool of your tool."

Consider this book a pill bottle for your leadership confidence. This experience will be delivered in doses so that you can partake, meditate and establish the principles to suit your life's framework. I'm excited to share this project with you and I'm honored that you have given me permission to fill in the gaps for you.

SECTION ONE |

CONFIDENCE

Possessing confidence is a prerequisite to leadership. With it, you can accomplish exploits that exceed your natural ability. Without it, the probability of you reaching your full potential is slim. I would venture to say that most people have struggled with their confidence at some point. And I dare not project that my confidence has never been crippled. On the contrary, I have been influenced by lower-level thinking on occasion.

Opportunities have slipped through my hands because I lacked the confidence to grab a hold to them. I didn't think I was good enough to maintain them. I was afraid that I would be judged by those who seemed more qualified than I was. But it was because I've conceded to fear that I know how to face it whenever it demonstrates that it still exist. Where there is fear, there is uncertainty. I don't know anybody who thrives in uncertainty. I've determined that confidence is not the absence of fear, but the ability to decide that the experience of engaging with it is greater than the uncertainty.

Eleanor Roosevelt believed that, "...you gain strength, courage, and confidence by every experience in which you really stop to look fear in the face. You are able to say to yourself, 'I lived through this horror. I can take the next thing that comes along'."

Moses was afraid to agree with Gods evaluation of his ability to save a nation from slavery. Abraham had reservations about his ability to produce and his wife's ability to conceive. Most entrepreneurs go through a phase of doubt even though they are confident in their business plan. How is it that we can be equipped for the job, have the resources to do that job, but remain apprehensive about performing it?

My friend, I submit to you that the absence of true confidence is the deciding metric that keeps us from excelling. True confidence takes the risk and is willing to absorb the fall. True confidence appreciates the preparation but needs to feel the impact of the moment to test itself against the market. True confidence needs to do the work instead of just talking about the work. When you possess real confidence you believe that God hears your requests.

My prayer is that you study this section well and use these principles and scriptures to activate your true confidence.

"God is calling you to a personal revolution. This is not the time to drag your feet. Tomorrow is not promised. Today is your day. Seize the moment."

Proverbs 1:22-33

"Leadership is all-inclusive."

Romans 11:28-29

"Your personal revolution pleads for you to live above the call of your flesh."

Romans 8:5-8

"Don't complain. Your words are powerful. You are not a victim. Cast your energy toward developing a solution."

Ephesians 4:29

"What God has equipped you with, you can conquer with. Your victory rests in what you have in your hands. You have been outfitted with all you need to be successful."

1 Samuel 17:39-40

"God has given you tools to bring forth the brilliance that is inside of you, so that He will get the glory out of your service."

Exodus 4:1-5

"You are a resource. You attract wealth and you distribute it. Be careful not to discount the significance you bring to the table."

Deuteronomy 28:13

"You have been chosen to author great exploits. Don't sabotage your success by playing small."

Jonah 1:1-3

LEADERSHIP ACTIVATION

Despite my inadequacies, I deserve to be here. Although I have failed, I can maximize my opportunities by not playing small. God is my confidence and I am more than capable of accomplishing the assignment that He has intended for me. I am equipped with everything I need to exceed even my own expectations of success.

SECTION TWO |

SPIRITUAL MATURITY

One of the joys of fatherhood is having the opportunity to directly impact my children's life. I couldn't imagine not being a constant presence for them. The habits that I create and the environment that my wife and I foster provides insight into the world outside of our home and shapes the way they will frame the world for themselves. It is true that parents are the child's first mentor and we have the awesome responsibility to influence their conscious and subconscious mind.

Before I leave for work in the morning I usually stand in front of our full body length mirror to make sure that I'm looking presentable. Little did I know that my son, who was only one year's old at the time, had picked up on my routine. On this particular morning he beat me to my spot and began playing with his reflection in the mirror by rocking left to right. He seemed to be having a good time so I stood back and watched him enjoy his moment of bliss. A few seconds passed before I decided to approach the mirror. As I began to walk up behind him he saw my reflection, stopped rocking and aligned himself with me.

Our relationship with God is similar to this.

As we try to find our way, God is watching us in support. When we finally align our will with His, we will start to see who we can become. Being able to identify our own spiritual growth is powerful. Five signs that you are growing spiritually are:

1. **You have an appetite for meat.** Simply put, you aren't concerned with just getting an

emotional high from a religious experience. You want to know how to live God's word in your daily life.

2. **You are not easily offended**. Being emotionally and mentally stable is the hallmark of a mature leader.

3. **You let the word of God decide your conscience**. When faced with decisions, tough or otherwise, you have less of a tendency to lean on your own understanding. God's word is your guiding post.

4. **You give God credit for your growth**. When you understand the power of God's grace and His forgiveness you will have no problem lifting up your trophies to Him. Just as Jesus fed the 5,000 with five loaves and two fish, God can multiply the little that you have and make it more than enough.

5. **You can celebrate the success of others.** Are you willing to be genuinely happy for others when they succeed? If so, you are living out the core of Philippians 2:4. Take a moment to read this passage to test your motives.

That is the fundamental framework and the level of spiritual maturity that causes us to live in purpose and activate the better version of ourselves.

"There will be some who can't comprehend the magnitude of what God has ordained over your life. They may try to dilute your assignment because of their lack of spiritual understanding. Keep moving forward"

Mark 6:11

"Don't dodge the hard experiences. Embrace them. Overcome your fears by using God's word as your weapon and your faith as a shield to absorb the blows of life."

Ephesians 6:13-17

"Survey your life to see what areas are fallow and begin to break up that ground. You will get dirty, but you just might discover something of value."

Hosea 10:12

"Self-confrontation is necessary to mature your perspective and increase your capacity to influence people."

2 Corinthians 13:5

"The relentless reframing of your thinking will keep you from duplicating the substandard results that you so desperately want to escape."

Philippians 4:8

"Everyone has obstacles to overcome. You can't hide from them. The beauty is in how you fight through them and eventually overcome them."

Romans 8:37

"Don't be afraid to commit to the rigor of development."

Proverbs 13:4

"Find value in the teachable moments of your obstacles. Everything happens for a reason. Open yourself up to the lesson of the obstacle."

1 Thessalonians 5:18

"We serve a God who loves us unconditionally and His grace is sufficient. However, His will is not suggestive. We do not serve a suggestive God and we are not fighting a suggestive enemy."

Exodus 20:1-7

"Sometimes, the best opportunities require the deepest sacrifice."

John 3:16

"Some leaders are born. Others are developed. Both need help to increase their capacity."

Proverbs 27:17

"Hearing from God should mean more to you than gaining the approval of your contemporaries."

John 5:43-44

"Don't let your ambition take you to a place you aren't ready for."

Matthew 16:26

LEADERSHIP ACTIVATION

To become the leader I was called to be, I am required to confront myself daily. The regular reframing of my thinking will push me closer to better results. When my leadership ideas are challenged, I will not dodge the hard decisions. As I develop, sacrifice is essential and patience is indispensible.

SECTION THREE |

RELATIONSHIPS

In chapter 3 of my book, *Lead With No Apologies: 21 Ways to Boost Your Influence* I talk about the importance of connecting to the right people. In that chapter I shared a few key questions that you should ask yourself to identify those who could help you get the best results. Here are a few of them:

- What do I need from this partner?
- Do they have the resources to support the vision?
- What are their expectations of me?

I once heard a speaker say that we must distinguish between those who are assigned to us and those who are attached to us. Those who are assigned to you have the capacity to fuel you up when you're empty and correct you when you're off track. Those who are attached to you may be good people but might not be equipped to help you reach your next level of leadership.

This is more of a cautionary appeal to you than an indictment on them. I had to learn this lesson the hard way. Understand who is assigned to help you and who isn't because sometimes our expectations can exceed their ability to deliver and that's not fair to them.

Many relationships have been destroyed for this very reason. A person may look the part but might not have the capacity to play the part. When this occurs it can cause frustration, resentment and a wasted opportunity for both you and the other person to be effective.

"When you understand that you are worth the work, you will soon find that some of your relationships and habits don't have the aptitude to support your reformed philosophy of success."

Proverbs 13:20

"The people we choose to invite into our destiny space can determine if we fulfill it or not."

I Corinthians 15:33

"Place yourself in environments that can help break up your unproductive views and awaken your passion to produce great things."

Psalms 1:1

"The level of your influence is contingent upon the types of partnerships you have."

Ecclesiastes 4:9-12

"Your associations, whether casual or intimate, will either breathe life into you or contribute to your demise."

I Thessalonians 5:11

"Supporters ride in the car with you, but Contributors give you gas money. Anybody can take a trip with you, but very few people are willing to share in the sacrifice of getting you to your destination."

Ruth 1:17

LEADERSHIP ACTIVATION

I promise to be more selective when building relationships. My partners are stakeholders in my destiny. Therefore, I will be careful to lend my time to those who appreciate my gift, challenge my perspectives and ideas and have the ability to support my endeavors. I will also add value to their lives in the same way.

SECTION 4 |

INFLUENCE

In a 2002 ESPN interview, baseball radio announcer, Ernie Harwell, was asked about one of the principles he shared in his Hall of Fame induction speech in 1981. In the speech he quoted the following line from the poem "Ulysses", written by Lord Tennyson.

"I am part of all that I have met."

When asked to elaborate, he said, "Everybody we meet has an influence on us and an impact - good or bad. And I think that's why we have to be careful with the way we handle people because what we're doing is making an impact."

Your influence is measured by your capacity to affect the character, development and behavior of others. Whether that impact is received as positive or negative is solely dependent on your motives and expected outcomes. Influence is a tool. Influence has the power to connect people. It is the reward given by those who feel empowered enough to offer it in exchange for your leadership.

Executing your power for selfish gain is easy, but the true test of your character is when you are willing to respond to the call of self-sacrifice. When you are confident enough to put your pride on the line for the benefit of others, that action breeds trust. And when trust and time conceive, influence is born and your impact becomes eternal.

"A large portion of your purpose is to shine so bright that the world is compelled to shine because of God's presence in you."

Matthew 5:14-15

*"No gift is too small. No tool is insignificant.
Your experience will generate
a spring of influence."*

Luke 21:1-4

"Your territory is your place of influence. It is the area that God has given you to nurture your gifts so that you can bless His people."

1 Peter 4:10

"Today, make a destiny decision. A destiny decision transcends the sensation of the moment. It forces you to reach into your future and compels you to get outside of yourself so that you can see the world from the perspective of your potential."

Ephesians 2:10

"Your life experiences give you the content to share with someone else that may be confronted with the same obstacle that you've overcome. Your experiences are someone else's solution."

Romans 3:23-24

"The culture that you create is the culture you will have to manage."

1 Samuel 2:22-25

"To influence fundamental change, a leader must project self-confidence and inspire his followers to subscribe to the higher version of themselves."

Luke 22:24-27

"Position yourself as a resource and watch resources start to come your way."

Deuteronomy 15:6-10

LEADERSHIP ACTIVATION

Because I have decided to shine, other leaders will have the courage to dominate in their domain of influence. I find teachable moments in my challenges that position me as a solution rather than a victim. My influence is an extension of God's influence, my potential is endless and my destiny is sure. I am a resource and I am significant.

SECTION 5 |

VISION & PURPOSE

Vision and purpose are related; you can't have one without the other. They go hand in hand. If vision means that you have made up in your mind that you will not quit until you've reached your goal, purpose is what allows you to stay focused on your goal despite the challenges that may arise.

More than the ability to see what others can't see, vision is having the capacity to notice when your plans are not working and the flexibility to edit your strategy. Purpose reminds you to readjust your attitude so that you can move forward with confidence.

These two powerful forces are ever present. Fighting for your attention are the options of being indolent or persistent. Keep in mind that lazy habits produce little fruit, while persistent behavior produces a life of accomplished goals and fulfillment.

Vision and purpose are at the forefront of you activating your leadership. You can try to institute all of the other principles, but without these two you will find yourself spinning your wheels, frustrated and unable to attain the clarity that you deserve.

Imagine driving in a rainstorm and all you can see are the lights from the other cars. Vision and purpose are like the windshield wipers on your car that help you see more clearly so that you can stay in your lane and reach your destination safely.

"Sometimes it's hard to digest what God has revealed to us because it may go against our corrupted view of success, cultural norms, and our self-built empires. "

Luke 18:18-23

"Cultivating your territory demands more than you wishing and hoping that things would get better; you are responsible for taking action. Fostering destiny involves thoughtful effort."

James 2:14-17

"What you want to become depends on your willingness to become it."

James 1:2-4

"Patience pays off. While your waiting for your breakthrough, be diligent in the small things."

Galatians 6:9

"The ability to lead positive change depends on one's personal conviction and their willingness to sacrifice luxury for legacy."

2 Timothy 4:6-8

*"As you grow in leadership,
so will your desires."*

1 Corinthians 13:11

"When God shows you something that you're supposed to do, start preparing for it."

Habakkuk 2:2

"What do you really want from life? If it's worth anything, it's not going to be cheap."

Hebrews 11:17

"Being used by God doesn't always feel good. Anything that is on display is open to judgment and ridicule."

2 Corinthians 12:10

"What God wants to do in your life is unimaginably unconventional."

Jeremiah 29:11

"Greatness is attracted to a renewed mind and seeks out the heart that is ready for the journey."

Revelation 3:20

"The purpose of your gifts and talents is to produce glory for God."

Colossians 3:23

"Sometimes all we need to do is simplify our lives. Forfeiting your agenda isn't always going to feel comfortable, but you must begin to live your life as a human being not just a human doing."

Mark 10:21

"You are alive to complete an assignment that is bigger than you."

Acts 20:35

"You are important to God and His Kingdom. Somebody is waiting to be blessed through you."

Galatians 5:13-14

LEADERSHIP ACTIVATION

I believe that I am an exceptional leader. I hear from God, apply His statutes to my life and live them out unashamedly. I was created for more than what I've experienced. I understand that God's presence is worth more than my performance. Lives will be changed because I know how to manage God's influence. I am diligent, obedient and available to be used by God; even if I have to stand alone.

CONCLUSION

Thank you for committing to your leadership development. Because you've invested in yourself, I believe that you have a genuine desire to lead unapologetically and increase your influence. There is something to be said about a leader who is authentic. I've always believed that truth is not afraid of questions, nor does it have to defend itself. It just is.

The same applies to leaders who are genuine. Leaders are constantly being watched, picked apart, and evaluated. Always remember that those who are influenced by you can sense when you aren't being sincere. Leaders must have a degree of transparency if they want to effectively engage with their team. Your commitment to helping them develop links them to you; the absence of genuine leadership leads to mistrust. Anything less than the truth is a mismanagement of your influence. Will you make mistakes? Yes, you absolutely will; that's part of your growth. But true leaders possess the courage to admit when they have been inconsistent, and the capacity to course correct themselves. As you lead unapologetically, do it with a grace that causes your team to see Jesus and a tenacity that provokes the world to be inspired to do the same.

ACTIVATE your confidence today!

WALK LIKE A KING

The Young Man's Guide To Conquering The World

LEAD WITH NO APOLOGIES

21 Ways To Boost Your Influence

Find More Leadership Resources At
www.JesseSpeaks.com